EXTREMELY *Weird* ANIMALS
AYE-AYE

BY LISA OWINGS

BELLWETHER MEDIA · MINNEAPOLIS, MN

Jump into the cockpit and take flight with Pilot books. Your journey will take you on high-energy adventures as you learn about all that is wild, weird, fascinating, and fun!

This edition first published in 2014 by Bellwether Media, Inc.

No part of this publication may be reproduced in whole or in part without written permission of the publisher. For information regarding permission, write to Bellwether Media, Inc., Attention: Permissions Department, 5357 Penn Avenue South, Minneapolis, MN 55419.

Library of Congress Cataloging-in-Publication Data

Owings, Lisa, author.
  Aye-aye / by Lisa Owings.
      pages cm. – (Pilot. Extremely Weird Animals)
  Summary: "Engaging images accompany information about aye-ayes. The combination of high-interest subject matter and narrative text is intended for students in grades 3 through 7"– Provided by publisher.
  Audience: Ages 7-12.
  Includes bibliographical references and index.
  ISBN 978-1-62617-073-5 (hardcover : alk. paper)
  1. Aye-aye–Juvenile literature. I. Title.
  QL737.P935O95 2014
  599.8'3–dc23
                    2013036455

Printed in the United States of America, North Mankato, MN.

TABLE OF CONTENTS

FINGER FOOD

The sun sinks below the trees on the island of Madagascar. Soon the aye-aye wakes and leaves its nest. Like a small monkey, the aye-aye scurries through the treetops. Suddenly, it stops climbing and wraps one hand around a branch. Then it brings its face close to the bark and raises its other hand.

The aye-aye extends its long, bony middle finger. It makes a series of quick taps on the bark and listens carefully with its sensitive ears. It can hear tasty **grubs** wiggling in the hollow tunnels beneath the bark. The aye-aye chews through the bark in just a few bites. It pokes its long finger into the hole and pulls out a fat grub. Slurp! It licks the juices from its hand. Then it begins looking for another meal.

ONE OF A KIND

The aye-aye is a small **mammal** with dark fur and an odd jumble of features. It has a bushy tail like a squirrel. Its hands could be a monkey's, but its long fingers are tipped with claws like a bird of prey. Its round, golden eyes look like an owl's. Above them spread the oversized ears of a bat.

primates

human   ape   monkey   lemur

Family Ties

Most primates have large brains, flat fingernails, and gently rounded back teeth. Sound familiar? That is because humans are primates, too. Humans are distant relatives of the aye-aye!

Daubentoniidae

aye-aye

When the aye-aye was discovered around 1780, scientists were unsure how to classify it. At first, they thought this unique creature was a rodent. Later, they found it had more in common with lemurs, monkeys, and apes. They decided the aye-aye was a primate. Still, the aye-aye didn't seem to fit with any of the existing groups of primates. It was one of a kind. So scientists made a new primate family called Daubentoniidae. The aye-aye is

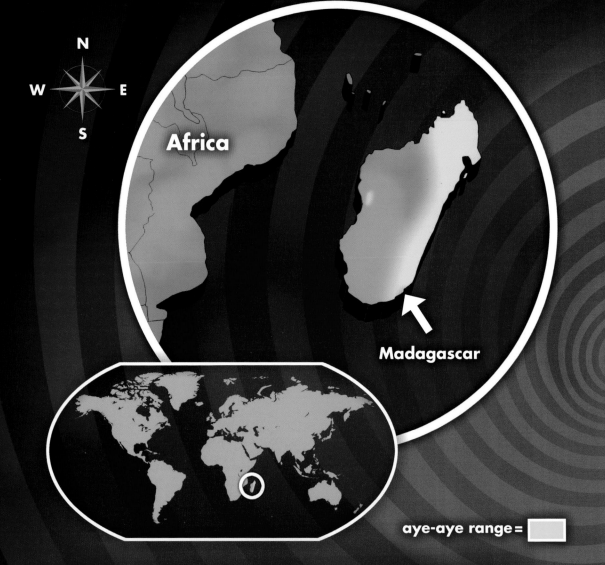

N
W E
S

Africa

Madagascar

aye-aye range =

Wild aye-ayes are found in only one place on Earth. They live on the island of Madagascar. This country sits about 250 miles (400 kilometers) off the southeastern coast of Africa. Most aye-ayes live in the rain forests of eastern Madagascar. However, they can also be found in other forests and on farms with fruit trees. Aye-ayes are very adaptable. They can live just about anywhere with trees.

Aye-ayes spend most of their lives in trees. During the day, they sleep in treetop nests made of leaves and branches. When night comes, the search for food begins. Aye-ayes eat mainly fruits and insect larvae. Eggs and nuts are other favorites. Aye-ayes often travel more than a mile (1.6 kilometers) each night. They explore the forest alone and return to their nests before dawn.

Solo Climbers
Aye-ayes usually avoid one another except when looking for a mate.

The aye-aye's tail is not just long. It is also big and fluffy. Its hairs can measure more than 9 inches (23 centimeters) long!

Adult aye-ayes usually weigh around 5 pounds (2 kilograms). Most are between 12 and 16 inches (30 and 41 centimeters) long from nose to **rump**. Their tails are several inches longer than their bodies. Aye-ayes sleep with their tails curled around them for warmth. Long tails also help them keep their balance as they move through the trees.

human

aye-aye

High in the treetops, aye-ayes have little to fear from predators. The cat-like fossa sometimes climbs up to snatch an aye-aye. However, humans are the aye-aye's main predator. Farmers kill aye-ayes to keep them from eating their crops. Many Madagascar **natives** also kill aye-ayes because they believe the animals are evil or bad luck. They think spotting one means someone will die. Aye-ayes may look strange, but they are not evil. They are simply misunderstood.

fossa

FROM FREAKY FINGERS TO EERIE EYES

One of the aye-aye's weirdest features is the middle finger on each hand. The finger is long and thin, just skin over bone. A ball-and-socket joint allows the aye-aye to move this finger in almost any direction. It can even fold it back against its hand! The aye-aye uses its special middle finger to find and eat food.

The finger is especially useful for finding larvae that tunnel beneath the bark of Madagascar's trees. The aye-aye taps the bark with its thin finger. It listens to the sound the taps make. Aye-ayes seem to be able to tell where the larvae are by tapping and listening. This is a form of echolocation. It is similar to the way bats use sound to "see" their world. The aye-aye may be the only primate to use echolocation to find food.

Super Senses

Most experts agree that the aye-aye finds larvae mainly by listening for them. Yet the aye-aye's nose is also powerful, and its finger is highly sensitive to touch. The aye-aye may use all these senses to find food.

Once the aye-aye finds a larva tunnel, it guides its finger down into it. The aye-aye feels around for a larva. Then it uses the finger's sharp claw like a fishing hook. It pulls the larva out and into its mouth. The aye-aye also uses its middle finger to scoop out the insides of nuts, fruits, and eggs. The finger can move from an aye-aye's food to its mouth around three times per second!

Studies have shown that the aye-aye's middle finger stays cooler than most other body parts when not in use. This helps the aye-aye save energy. The animal warms up the finger when searching for food. When walking or climbing, the aye-aye keeps this finger folded back. This protects the delicate tool from injury.

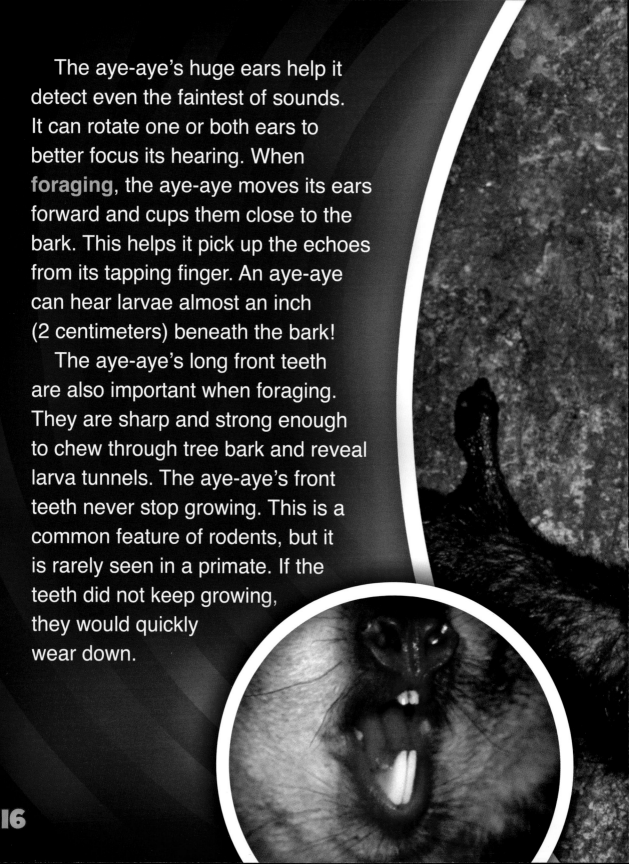

The aye-aye's huge ears help it detect even the faintest of sounds. It can rotate one or both ears to better focus its hearing. When foraging, the aye-aye moves its ears forward and cups them close to the bark. This helps it pick up the echoes from its tapping finger. An aye-aye can hear larvae almost an inch (2 centimeters) beneath the bark!

The aye-aye's long front teeth are also important when foraging. They are sharp and strong enough to chew through tree bark and reveal larva tunnels. The aye-aye's front teeth never stop growing. This is a common feature of rodents, but it is rarely seen in a primate. If the teeth did not keep growing, they would quickly wear down.

Like a Woodpecker?

There are no woodpeckers in Madagascar, but aye-ayes find food in much the same way. Both animals knock on trees to find hollow spots. When they find such a spot, they make a hole in the tree and scoop out their prey.

17

It is hard to ignore the aye-aye's creepy stare. Its large, round eyes help it to find food at night. The eyes have a reflective layer in the back that helps the aye-aye see better in the dark. Another feature of the aye-aye's eyes is that they can see color even at night. Most mammals can see only in black and white in the dark.

Aye-ayes also have **nictitating membranes**, sometimes called third eyelids. These thin pieces of skin move across the eyes to keep them moist and clean. They are **transparent** enough to let in light. Although nictitating membranes are common in **reptiles** and birds, they are hardly ever found in primates. Some experts believe these membranes protect the aye-aye's eyes from flying bits of wood while it chews through trees.

A Big Brainiac

The aye-aye's brain is larger than that of any of its close relatives, such as lemurs and lorises. This brain structure helps the aye-aye make sense of all the information coming from its eyes, ears, nose, and fingers.

ADAPTING TO CHANGE

For a long time, the aye-aye was considered endangered. However, scientists discovered in 2008 that aye-ayes were less at risk than they thought. The animals could be found almost everywhere in Madagascar. Today, aye-ayes are listed as near threatened. That means they may become endangered in the future. People are destroying their forests, and many still kill them. More and more aye-ayes die each year because of these threats.

Many people are working to keep aye-ayes safe. In 1966, several aye-ayes were moved to Nosy Mangabe, a small island off the eastern coast of Madagascar. This reserve is one of at least 16 areas across Madagascar where aye-ayes are protected. Aye-ayes are also bred and cared for in zoos around the world. This means more people can see and learn about the wonderfully weird aye-aye!

EXTINCT

EXTINCT IN THE WILD

CRITICALLY ENDANGERED

ENDANGERED

VULNERABLE

NEAR THREATENED

LEAST CONCERN

Aye-Aye Fact File

Common Name: aye-aye

Scientific Name: *Daubentonia madagascariensis*

Famous Features: long middle finger, long front teeth, golden eyes, huge ears, bushy tail

Distribution: Madagascar

Habitats: rain forests, other forests, farms with fruit trees

Diet: insect larvae, fruits, nuts, eggs

Life Span: average of 20 years in captivity; the aye-aye's life span in the wild is unknown.

Current Status: near threatened

GLOSSARY

adaptable—able to adjust to a wide variety of conditions

bred—mated to produce young in captivity

classify—to assign something to a group based on common traits

echolocation—a way of locating objects by listening to echoes, or sound waves traveling back to the ears

endangered—at risk of becoming extinct

foraging—searching for food

grubs—insect larvae

larvae—insects that have just recently been born or hatched

mammal—an animal that has a backbone, hair, and feeds its young milk

natives—people who are originally from a specific place

nictitating membranes—clear inner eyelids that close to protect an aye-aye's eyes

primate—a member of a group of mammals that can use their hands to grasp food and other objects

rain forests—thick, green forests that receive a lot of rain

reptiles—cold-blooded animals with scaly skin such as snakes, lizards, and turtles

reserve—an area where animals are protected and cannot be hunted

rodent—a mammal with large, constantly growing front teeth; squirrels, beavers, and rats are examples of rodents.

rump—the hind end of a mammal

threats—possible dangers

transparent—clear, or letting light through

TO LEARN MORE

AT THE LIBRARY

Aronin, Miriam. *Aye-Aye: An Evil Omen*. New York, N.Y.: Bearport Pub., 2009.

Frazel, Ellen. *Madagascar*. Minneapolis, Minn.: Bellwether Media, 2013.

Throp, Claire. *Lemurs*. Chicago, Ill.: Heinemann Library, 2012.

ON THE WEB

Learning more about aye-ayes is as easy as 1, 2, 3.

1. Go to www.factsurfer.com.

2. Enter "aye-ayes" into the search box.

3. Click the "Surf" button and you will see a list of related Web sites.

With factsurfer.com, finding more information is just a click away.

INDEX

The images in this book are reproduced through the courtesy of: imagebroker/ SuperStock, front cover, pp. 18-19; Minden Pictures/ SuperStock, pp. 4, 5, 11; blickwinkel/ Schmidbauer/ Alamy, p. 6; Mint Images/ Glow Images, pp. 9, 17; NHPA/ SuperStock, pp. 10, 13, 14; Nick Garbutt/ SuperStock, p. 15; Thomas and Pat Leeson/ Science Photo Library/ ScienceSource, p. 16; Brian Lasenby, p. 17 (small); David Haring/ DUPC/ Getty Images, p. 21.